'One Body... Many Members'

Philip J. Anderson

The Covenant Church in Historical Perspective

cp
covenant press
3200 west foster avenue
chicago, illinois 60625
312-478-4676

Copyright © 1983, Covenant Press
ISBN 0-910452-53-9

CONTENTS

The Evangelical Covenant Church in Historical Setting	1
Beginnings	3
The Early Church	5
The Medieval Church	11
The Reformation	19
The Evangelical Awakenings	25
The Covenant Church in North America	29
Suggestions for Further Reading	33

Foreword

This important resource comes from Covenant Press in response to a felt need in the churches for a brief sketch of the body of Christ that would set the Evangelical Covenant Church in historical perspective.

Covenant Affirmations, earlier available in tract, booklet, and full-length book form, came in response to similar queries about what the Covenant Church believes and how it relates theologically to other branches on the vine that is Christ's body.

We are grateful to Dr. Philip J. Anderson, assistant professor of church history at North Park Theological Seminary, both for his willingness to provide us with this resource and the spirit in which he has done his work. We are also indebted to David Westerfield, art editor of *The Covenant Companion*, for the design, layout, and illustrations.

James R. Hawkinson
Executive Secretary of
Covenant Publications
June, 1983

THE EVANGELICAL COVENANT CHURCH IN HISTORICAL SETTING

Seen from a distance, the Church is something like an ancient majestic oak. Its limbs branch off, some straight and true, some twisted and gnarled, some healthy and budding with life, some dry and lifeless. Despite the marvelous appearance of the tree in all its variety, its roots are planted firmly and deeply in the soil. Though we may speak of many churches and denominations, as Christians we believe there is only one Church, one undivided body of Christ. All strive to serve one Master and tell faithfully the story of salvation.

The Church is the Christian's spiritual home. One scarcely can travel through any village, town, or city in the Western world and not find the horizon marked by the slender steeple or square tower of a church. In America, it is not uncommon to drive through a neighborhood of a large city and pass a variety of churches: Catholic, Episcopal, Lutheran, Presbyterian, Methodist, Orthodox, Baptist—to mention only the largest and most historic. The physical presence of the Church is everywhere. The traditions of belief and practice in each church, however, embody the fact that historic Christianity has expressed itself in many ways: the meditative silence of a Quaker meetinghouse in rural England and high mass at

'One Body . . . Many Members'

St. Peter's Cathedral in Rome; the withdrawal of an Egyptian hermit from the world and the long days of a Salvation Army worker in an urban ghetto; the percussive chant of a tribe in Zaire and the glorious "Hallelujah Chorus" from Handel's *Messiah;* the simplicity of a Franciscan monk in his cell and the worldly pomp of a Renaissance pope on his throne; the self-giving service of Mother Teresa in India and the glitter and polish of an American T.V. evangelist.

Some of us have been aware of the Christian Church from our earliest memories. Perhaps our parents brought us to the Church as tiny infants and presented us confidently to God or made baptismal vows on our behalf, placing us in the care and nurture of a congregation of believers. Some of us have never left the fold of the Church, while some, like prodigal sons or daughters, have wandered away for a season only to be drawn back by God's redeeming grace into renewed fellowship. Others have never known the Church until a life-changing encounter with the Gospel of Christ made them, by definition, a part of this eternal reality on earth. The experience of each individual has varied and we are all too prone to base our understanding of the Church on that experience. While this is only natural, it is also confining and means that our knowledge is fragmentary and sometimes ill-conceived. The Church not only has the gospel story to tell; it also has a wonderful story of its own life—an instructive and edifying story of God's activity in the midst of his people throughout history.

In this booklet, I have sketched the general outlines of the Church's history. I hope readers will see the oneness of the Evangelical Covenant Church with the universal Church, and how it compares with some other religious traditions. Our heritage and beliefs are much older than the founding of the denomination in 1885, yet we have an identity which both sets us apart from and complements the rich variety of churches that composes the united body of Christ in the world. This booklet is only a beginning. It will not answer all the reader's questions, but will have served its purpose if it encourages a desire to learn more about the Covenant and its place in the history of the Christian Church.

BEGINNINGS

The Church is the body of Christ and therefore has its beginnings with the life and ministry of Jesus of Nazareth. The birth of the Church was the fulfillment of God's promises to his people in the Old Testament, part of the inauguration of a new age in the teaching, death, and resurrection of our Lord.

Our story begins in the time of Jesus almost two thousand years ago. As we read the New Testament, however, we become aware of the continuity of thought and life between it and the story of God's relationship with his people in the Old Testament. There is a connection between promise and fulfillment in the redemptive activity of God. While it is always the same God who speaks, at a particular moment in time he began to speak in a new way, not through prophets but through a Son.

The first thirty years of Jesus' life were spent in obscurity in the village of Nazareth where he, like his father, became a carpenter. Following his baptism by a prophet named John, who spoke of a new age to come, Jesus began teaching in the northern part of Palestine. The people heard him with glad hearts because he made religion more simple and sensible by giving up the excessive petty rules of the Jewish law. But he did not make religion any easier, for he upheld the heart of Jewish law and even went beyond it in teaching all people to forgive wrongs and love enemies. He gathered huge crowds as he spoke words of life, criticized selective keepers of the law who neglected its weightier matters, warned the wealthy, performed miracles, and healed the sick. Some even wanted to make him a king.

Jesus gathered around him a small yet diverse group of followers called to be "fishers of men." They observed firsthand the marvelous work of their Master and learned little by little the true purpose of his life and ministry. In fact, they came to recognize him as the Son of God. They soon realized, however, that Jesus was not going to take up weapons against the enemy, but would build up his kingdom in the hearts of people like themselves. These disciples were the nucleus of the Christian Church. Surely they were disillusioned and badly frightened when Jesus suffered and died on the cross as a religious and political troublemaker. Many even lost faith in their Lord's promises. But, as he had said, he was raised from the dead on the third day and appeared first to Mary Magdalen and Peter and then to others, filling that tiny community with new hope and firm assurance that all that Jesus had taught and promised was true.

Before his ascension, Jesus promised to send his Spirit as Comforter to guide the apostles in the challenging work of the great commission that lay before them. On the day commonly called Pentecost, this small band of followers was dramatically empowered by the Holy Spirit. It was an event of sacred history in which the disciples were invested with an authority and power that made them preachers and dispensers of the riches of the risen Christ. The number of Christ's followers increased dramatically that day. Perhaps most importantly, the Spirit of God fused the many into one fellowship of divine love. The Church often refers to Pentecost Sunday in worship as its birthday, and this should be so. It is more accurate to say, however, that the beginning of the Church is to be found in the combination of these events, and that its foundation is the person and work of Christ. This is history. But the earliest Christians believed, as we do today, that the ultimate origin of the Church lies beyond the realm of history in the eternal providence of God, that in his grace he has loved us and chosen us to be his own. These first Christians believed that the Church was a divine creation of grace, indwelt by the Holy Spirit, whose presence gave life and meaning to their fellowship.

THE EARLY CHURCH

The period of the "early Church" covers about the first five centuries of the Church's history. During this time the Church spread throughout the Mediterranean world, giving rise to heresies and harsh persecution, as well as to a new generation of theologians who sought to defend the Church's life and thought. Differences of opinion on many fundamental issues of belief led to the formation of the New Testament canon, and to councils and creeds to set the limits of orthodox belief and practice. This was a time of fluid change, growth, institutionalization, and creative thinking in the Church. It was also a time of decay for the greatest of all ancient civilizations, the Roman Empire.

Who were the first Christians making up the Church after Pentecost? They were Jews, differentiated from their compatriots by their faith that in Jesus of Nazareth the Messiah, long expected, had now come. The apostles—those who had witnessed the risen Christ—spoke in their midst and in his name. The substance of their preaching, the core of the Gospel, comprised the following essentials. First, the promises of God in the Old Testament have now been fulfilled; the Messiah has come. Second, the Messiah is Jesus, who did good and mighty works by the power of God, was crucified according to the purpose of God, was raised by God from the dead, was exalted by God and given the name "Lord" (Psalm 110:1), and will come again for judgment and the restoration of all things. And finally, all who hear the message should believe, repent, and be baptized. The message was backed by the authority of the apostles and in succeeding generations this core became the criterion by which teachers and preachers were judged orthodox, and by which the writings in the New Testament were judged canonical and the Word of God.

The witness of the apostles as recorded in the Gospels and by Paul has remained the touchstone of the Church's teaching, though interpreted in different ways by Catholics and Protestants. The Roman Catholic tradition has depended on the office of bishop beginning with Peter for the apostolic—and therefore authoritative—witness to the Gospel. The Covenant Church, however, following in the Reformation and free church traditions, believes that the continuity of the faithful preaching of the Word and the practice of the sacraments are what keep us faithful to the apostles' witness, and in true apostolic succession.

The first Christians were judged by their fellow Jews to be members of a radical Messianic Jewish sect. For this reason we must view the primitive Christian community in Jerusalem as part of the general context of its contemporary Judaism. This community was headed by James, the brother of Jesus, and was committed to the Jewish promised land, faithful to the cult of the Temple, and strictly observant of Mosaic practices. They circumcized their male infants and followed rites of purification, kept the Sabbath, and took part in the prayers recited daily at the Temple. But these early Christians attended the Temple as a group and found their deeper identity in *ecclesia*, the Greek word for church which means "those who are called out." They combined their synagogue worship with the upper room teaching of Jesus, and met often in private homes for a meal, the Lord's Supper, instruction, prayer, and praise. In all, their lives were filled with the hope of Christ's return, and they pooled their material resources to help each other and to witness to the world while they awaited that happy event.

Christianity spread far and wide during the first fifteen years. Soon, Antioch became the second center of the Church along with Jerusalem. This was a cosmopolitan city of Greek culture and political importance as the legal center of the eastern province of the Roman Empire. Many Jews and Gentiles were converted there in the decade following Christ's resurrection. In fact, the name "Christian" was first applied in Antioch as a political term (Acts 11:26). Problems quickly arose. Antioch was the starting point of the mission to Asia, and Jewish and Gentile Christians in the city formed separate communities, dividing over the necessity of maintaining Jewish law, and refusing to share the Lord's Supper together. The book of Acts and Paul's letter to the Galatians record these struggles and the eventual triumph of the fact that Christianity is universal. The persistent efforts of Paul, Barnabas, Peter, and others insured that the expansion of the Church would be free from the legalisms of a narrow Jewish Christianity. The fall of Jerusalem in 70 A.D. all but put an end to the primacy and influence of the congregation in that city and meant that the immediate future of the Christian religion was to played out in non-Jewish, predominantly Greek lands.

The Church was launched into a world of widespread religious interest and much variety in religious options: loyalty to ancient deities, emperor worship, mystery religions which were ascetic, highly speculative, and philosophical. This was especially true as the Church expanded primarily in a world governed by Greek thought. It is not surprising that the apostolic core of the Christian religion, born in a Hebrew, oriental world, was seriously threatened. The most serious challenge of all came from the Gnostics, who believed that the individual was saved by right knowledge (*gnosis*). Little is known about the origins of Gnosticism, a highly philosophical religion, but its Greek cosmological mythology made deep inroads into the Christian faith—especially in Egypt, one of the areas where Christianity spread most rapidly. It denied the humanity of Jesus, seeking to preserve the deity of Christ, often rejected the God of the Old Testament as irreconcilable with the God of the New, and contrasted the goodness of the spiritual realm with the total baseness of everything in the material world. To the gnostic Christian, the creation of the world was a mistake, the work of some misguided lesser god, and only the knowledge brought by the divine Christ would ever lead the entrapped soul out of physical bondage back to its spiritual home. Paul and other leaders of the early Church were certainly familiar with Christians who adapted their new faith to such Greek ways of thinking, and they worked vigorously to maintain the purity of the Gospel.

This generalized illustration is but one example of many emerging "heresies"—beliefs the Church rejected because they seemed to undercut the salvation of the whole person or to distort its teach-

'One Body . . . Many Members'

ing. In response, the Church took the offensive in preserving orthodox doctrine, and much of its early theology was hammered out during the second century by church leaders known as "apologists." Since the Lord had not returned as expected, the Church had now to learn to live in the world, to stand its ground, and to defend itself using the thought forms and language of its Greek contemporaries. In addition to the problem of heresy, intense persecutions which cost many Christians their lives in Rome and other imperial cities—beginning with Nero's persecution in 64 until the time the first Christian emperor Constantine put an end to them in 313—forced the Church to develop its structures of worship, doctrine, order, and authority. It is ironic that the persecutions, designed to break the back of the upstart Christian religion by requiring emperor worship, only made believers more firm and tenacious in their faith, some even seeking martyrdom as a way of sharing in Christ's sufferings.

By the fourth century there were four great centers of Christianity—Rome, Constantinople, Antioch, and Alexandria. Differing ways of thinking about faith developed in these cities, and there was also much political intrigue involving secular and religious leaders, as Christianity by the Edict of Milan (313) became the official religion of the Roman Empire. During this time, the churches of the western half of the Mediterranean world held some significantly different theological opinions and operated in some different ways from the churches in the eastern half. Bishops in the more important cities were vying for prominence, and the special authority of the bishop of Rome—which later took the form of the papacy—was beginning to be felt. The most serious differences of theology in the fourth and fifth centuries existed between Alexandria in Egypt, Antioch in Palestine, and Constantinople in Asia Minor, over such fundamental issues as the relationship of the Father to the Son, the persons and relations within the Trinity, and the nature of Christ. How is it that Jesus Christ can be God? How can we speak of Father, Son, and Holy Spirit and still maintain the unity and oneness of the Godhead, a unique distinctive of the Judeo-Christian religion? What is the relationship of Christ's human nature to his divine nature? The general councils of Nicaea (325), Constantinople (381), Ephesus (431), and Chalcedon (451)—attended by politicians, church leaders, and theologians—were called to settle these disputes. The creeds that they agreed upon defined and set parameters of orthodoxy for generations of Christians to come, though controversy would and does continue on many of these questions.

The Early Church

The history of the early Church up to the end of the fifth century is a fascinating and rich period of belief and practice, in which catholicity came to mean the collective authority of Scripture (the New Testament canon as we know it was closed in 397), creed, and bishop. Much of our present understanding of the Church is derived from a knowledge and appreciation of this time as interpreted through our own understanding of Scripture. We owe an enormous debt to the early Church Fathers like Irenaeus, Origen, Athanasius, Tertullian, and Augustine, who gave us a framework of thought and a language in which to articulate our faith.

While the Covenant is "non-creedal" in that we do not make the words of the creeds or the utterances of the Fathers authoritative alongside of or above Scripture, nevertheless we affirm the fundamental expressions of faith in which Christians the world over are agreed, and stand with the apostolic witness of the ages whenever we confess our faith in the Apostles', Nicene, or Athanasian creeds.

THE MEDIEVAL CHURCH

The Middle Ages spanned roughly a thousand years, during which time the Church developed into the most powerful institution in Western civilization. Popes gained enormous power in both spiritual and temporal affairs, governing a church of escalating wealth and bureaucracy. Monks, nuns, and monastic houses became familiar sights in most cities and towns. Great universities were formed to support a highly integrated system of theology. Hospitals and other benevolent institutions were organized. Yet in all of this activity, an increasing number of people began to question what they believed to be the worldliness and corruption of the Church, and its apparent monopoly on grace through a sacramental structure that did not seem to encourage personal faith and devotion.

The history of the Western Church in the Middle Ages is the story of the most elaborate and thoroughly integrated system of religious thought and practice the world has ever known. The sacking of Rome by barbarians in 410 led eventually to a thousand years of rapid change in the development of European life and culture, a time when the outlines of our institutions and habits of

'One Body . . . Many Members'

thought were drawn in sharp relief. During the Middle Ages (roughly 500 to 1500), the Church became identified with the whole of organized society, a feature which distinguishes it from both earlier and later periods. The medieval period has been popularly described as the "Dark Ages," implying a rather extended time of backward stagnation in the history of the Church and human civilization. Certainly the chaos of a barbarian West along with a politically weak Church made for a bleak picture in the early years. To understand these thousand years and dispel the notion that it was all dark, however, it is much more helpful to speak of three different periods of development and change.

1) Prior to the middle of the eleventh century, most of western Europe struggled to maintain physical conditions supporting the basics of life. The fall of the Roman Empire left a spiritual and political ruin which took centuries to repair. The West was characterized by poverty, disease, and famine; there was little industry, agricultural knowledge and methods were primitive, and the small towns and rural areas were thinly populated. It was an age of superstition and ignorance. Compared with the remnants of Eastern Christianity and particularly the Muslim world—whose more learned and rich culture then dominated Asia Minor, Palestine, Egypt, and North Africa—the West seemed inferior. When the followers of Islam (in Arabic, "the way") invaded Europe, the West barely survived. Ceremony in both religion and politics became a means of stability through a physical association with eternal reality. The mass assumed great importance; through it the faithful actually touched the Lord's body. The physical relics of saints were cherished because ordinary people could see and handle them. The emperor Charlemagne, crowned by a pope in 800, had a huge hollow throne filled with human relics, and medieval kings wore them in their crowns and around their necks. Elaborate ceremony gave the impression of a majestic godly ruler, but it only disguised the most fragile component of medieval society.

Even in this seemingly dark period, however, there were indications of light. In time it appeared that the unitary authority of an imperial papacy in Rome was to be the foundation for rebuilding the fallen empire. Pope Gregory the Great (590-604) was the most learned man of his age and consolidated the power of the papacy in Italy, giving it universal vision and making it a moral force in politics. He systematized a body of doctrine and worship that endured for centuries. Rome was the city where Peter was martyred, and it was believed that his living voice guided the Church from the tomb

The Medieval Church

through the passive mouth of the pope, his Vicar. As that authority solidified, the popes also assumed the title of Supreme Temporal Lord over the affairs of church and state. Equally important, monasteries were living symbols of stability in a society characterized by flux. Monasteries patterned after the order of St. Benedict (b. 480) and his *Rule for Monks* (in turn derived from a well-established tradition of asceticism in the Eastern Church) became centers of learning, obedience, and spiritual formation, providing needed leadership in the Church. The elaborate liturgical routine of the Benedictines, in addition to the institution of tithes, the geographical organization of dioceses and parishes, and an unshakeable loyalty to Rome were all contributions during this first period of the Middle Ages that proved virtually indestructible. Moreover, after hundreds of years of wrangling over the question of supremacy, the Eastern and Western Churches separated officially in 1054 (the Great Schism) into the Roman Catholic and Eastern Orthodox communions; respective leaders leveled excommunications at one another that drove an immovable wedge between the two churches until 1964 when Pope Paul VI visited the Holy Land and met with the Patriarch of Constantinople, initiating the process of removing the sentences of excommunication.

2) The period from 1050 to 1300 marked the high point of the Middle Ages. The typical caricature of the medieval world as having its head in the clouds and one foot in the grave is anything but true. The evangelization of the European barbarian tribes—which still worshiped nature deities and followed other ancient ritual practices—was almost complete, and expanding frontiers were colonized. New towns were formed and economic development was unprecedented. Expert knowledge was required in all areas of life, and administration and specialization in the Church took the place of ritual as the chief instrument of government. The medieval Church became a great administrative machine of laws and law courts, taxes and tax collectors, and the manipulation of the power of life and death over people—for through the sacraments the Church was the sole dispenser of grace. The ideal Church of the time was a society of disciplined and organized clergy directing the thoughts and activities of an obedient and receptive laity—kings, magistrates, and peasants alike. Because of a monastic system which now included Augustinians, Cistercians, Dominicans, and Franciscans in competition with one another, the clergy had a clear monopoly on ability. The first universities at Paris, Bologna, Padua, Oxford, and Cambridge, spawned by the monastic movement,

became great intellectual centers of highly technical and philosophical "scholastic" theology—such as that of Anselm, Abelard, and Thomas Aquinas—which tightened the Church's authority by the development of canon law. The Church grew wealthy in property and material possessions, and through such powerful popes as Gregory VII (Hildebrand), temporal rulers were invested with what power they had. The popes now rejected the humbler title of Vicar of St. Peter for the more exalted one of Vicar of Christ.

The eleventh and twelfth centuries also saw the establishment of abbeys, nunneries, and hospitals in addition to schools, and the construction of the magnificent cathedrals of Europe, the greatest and most enduring symbols of the faith of the Middle Ages. It was also the exciting yet tragic time of the Crusades—great religious armies marching to Palestine to gain wealth and political power, and to reclaim holy places and relics from the Islamic worshipers of Allah. Popes granted indulgences, removing punishment for sin in the next life for those who organized, sponsored, and participated in the Crusades. In such blind enthusiasm, even a group of white-clad children marched off to their slaughter. Those who died in the Crusades were considered martyrs for Christ.

3) Despite this century and a half of irrepressible growth, inevitable seeds of unrest began to sprout, exposing corruption and legalism in the hierarchy of the Church. Scholastic dogma was undermined not only by new philosophies and the revival of old ones, but also by a blossoming mysticism which stressed a heightened spirituality and immediacy of experience. To many devout Christians—inspired by mystic leaders like Bernard of Clairveaux—prayer, meditation, contemplation, and mystical communion with God were more real and vital in the life of the believer than the Church's dispensary role in matters of sacramental grace, or the "scholastic" view that intellectual reason completes the revelation given in Scripture. The fourteenth and fifteenth centuries also witnessed the rise of popular religious movements in opposition to the worldliness and power of the papacy, part of a complex process in which the papacy declined as a political, moral, and spiritual force. Schism within the Church from 1309 to 1378 occurred when its central administration was moved from Rome to Avignon in France. The papacy never recovered fully from this political turmoil; and the new councils called to try to settle the issue further eroded the pope's authority, as greater numbers in the Church regarded such conciliar activity as holding authority at least equal to the pope's.

The Medieval Church

In various areas of Europe and England, new movements of reform spoke with strong voices and attracted large followings. In England during the fourteenth century, John Wycliffe and the Lollards endeavored to expel Italian clergy, criticized the Roman Catholic view of the Lord's Supper (that the bread and wine actually turn into Christ's body and blood), stressed the individual's personal relationship to God, and—through the work of Wycliffe—translated the entire Bible from Latin into English. In Bohemia during the following century, John Hus led a grass-roots movement which echoed Wycliffe's complaints, denounced indulgences, attacked the clergy for its laxity, and asserted that Christ, not the pope, was the true head of the Church. Hus paid for his views with his life. In Florence during the 1490s, the fiery Italian preacher, Savonarola, denounced the sins of the Church and called the pope and his cardinals and bishops back to the simplicity of the Gospel. He too was burned at the stake. In all of this, the stage was set for a sweeping reformation of the Church, one that would value and treasure that which was healthy in the medieval Church, yet would seek to recover the vitality and purity of New Testament faith and practice.

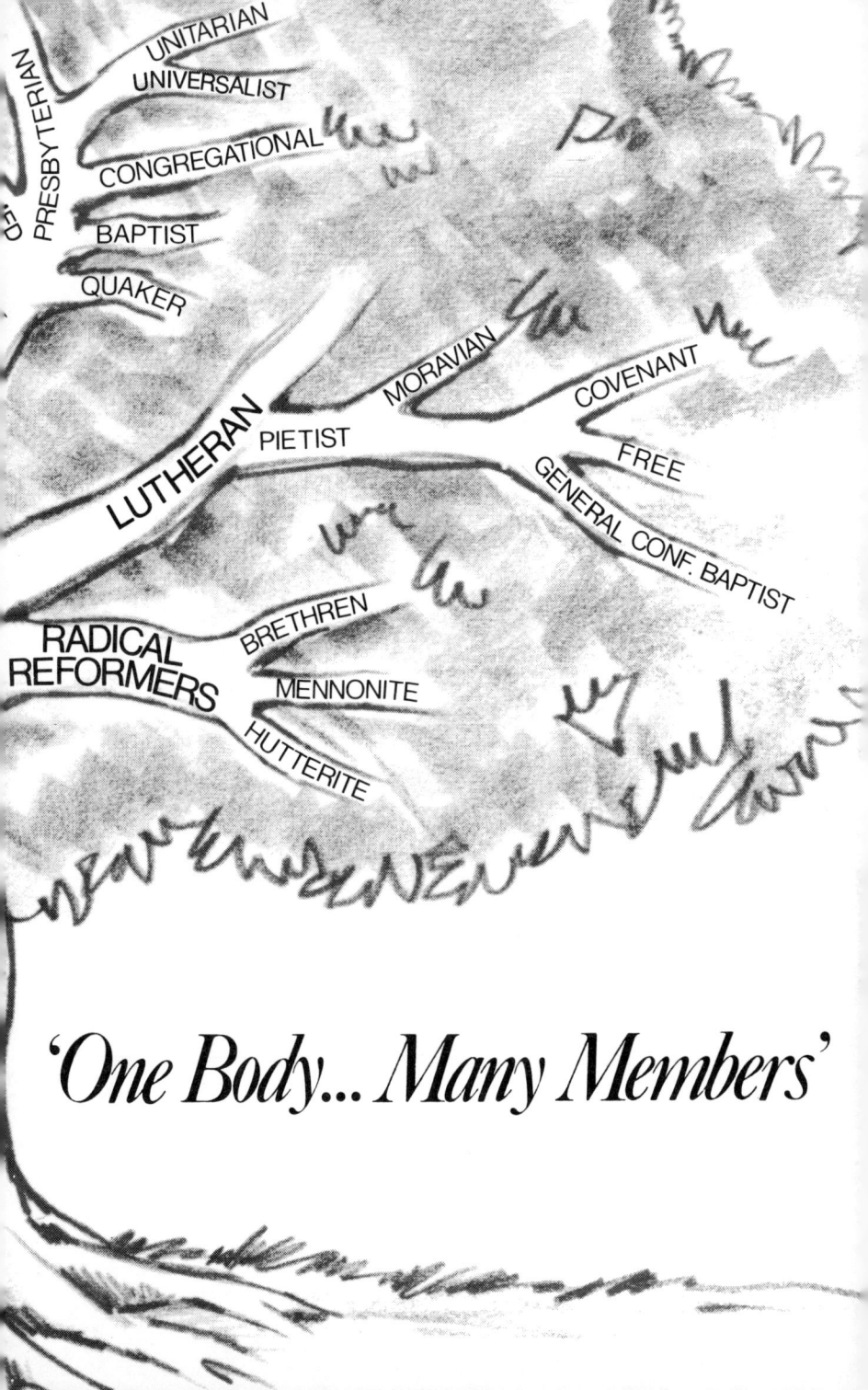

THE REFORMATION

Most of today's major Protestant denominations—Lutheran, Presbyterian, Baptist, Episcopal, Congregational—can be traced back to the people and events of the Reformation in the sixteenth century. Though it took different forms throughout Europe, England, and Scandinavia, the Reformation was based on many common principles derived from the Bible, which the reformers believed was the highest and only authority representing the mind of Christ. They sought to rid the Church of nonbiblical beliefs and practices, and to recover within the experience and knowledge of each person the meaning of sin and grace, faith and forgiveness.

The Reformation of the sixteenth century resulted in what we now call Protestantism (the term was first used in 1529 at the Diet of Speyer), a new dimension in the Church's history. Its most notable quality is diversity, recognizing that people think different thoughts even when they seek to witness to the same Gospel. Human creativity, finitude, and selfishness have always made the interpretation of right faith and order difficult, and have produced many perplexing ambiguities in the Church. What is distinctive about Protestantism is that it accepts these ambiguities as part of its heritage, as both a sign of health and a symptom of sickness. A Protestant must always seek to discern the difference. Such diversity has occurred because Protestantism has been a movement which consciously has assumed the burden of relating its message directly to the concerns and problems of people in specific historical contexts. Human problems may remain largely the same in all ages, but the questions have been asked in new ways and have demanded different kinds of solutions in each time and place, for the Church —like any other institution—has been shaped by its culture.

In the Protestant Reformation, however, diversity had a focus of unity in the principle of the supreme authority of the Bible. It is the message of the Bible that must be related to each particular situation. Protestants have emphasized the right of the individual to think his or her own thoughts, wherever they may lead, as long as his or her life and thinking take their cue from the message of Scripture, however differently that message is understood. Protestantism is the story of individuals and groups who have taken their understanding of the Gospel so seriously that they have been willing, if necessary, to create new forms of the Church; though it must be recognized that the reformers of the sixteenth century broke reluctantly with the Roman institution in order, they believed, to preserve its apostolic heritage. Protestantism, then, has to do not so much with a *church*, as in Roman Catholicism, but with a movement made up of *churches*, though both seek to understand the reality of the universal Church. Protestantism is a story to be told; it cannot be defined by a single religious concept.

We have already mentioned some of the forces that helped bring about the dissolutions of the one medieval Church. In addition to mysticism and early reformers, there were other developments even more far-reaching. The invention of the printing press by Johann Gutenberg about the year 1450, and his printing of the Latin Bible, led not only to the increased production of the biblical text but also to the wide dissemination of ideas. The revolutionary nature of this cannot be overemphasized. Also during this time, nationalistic loyalties were beginning to well up in the hearts of the people of Germany, France, England, and Switzerland. Cities became strong and economically stable, so that powerful local governing burghers were soon in conflict with the ambitions of princes and nobles who pressed for a national kingship; and, of course, most were in opposition to a pope and college of cardinals ruling their lands and people from Rome. A middle class was rising as well, as the traditional feudal system of nobles, lords, and serfs

The Reformation

crumbled so it is not surprising to find the territories of the Reformation embroiled in princely wars and peasant revolts. The most serious threat to papal supremacy came not from reformers' doctrine, but from the nationalism of secular rulers.

The Reformation cannot be interpreted apart from the influence of the Renaissance either. The late Middle Ages had also been a time of general intellectual and cultural renewal, when the lofty ideals of ancient Greece and Rome had been resurrected. This renewal, characterized by the term "humanism" (not to be confused with the narrow misuse of the term in our day), centered first in Italy and then spread northwards, promoting human artistic and literary creativity, and above all, the worth of the individual person. This new outlook was supported by popes like Sixtus IV, who erected the Sistine Chapel, and the warrior pope, Julius II, who, when not off leading his armies in battle, found time to be a patron to Raphael and Michelangelo. This spirit of classical learning encouraged the recovery of ancient texts and languages. The result was a vigorous study of the Bible in its original languages, with scholars like Johann Reuchlin establishing the Hebrew texts of the Old Testament, and Erasmus of Rotterdam—greatest of the Christian humanists—having the first Greek New Testament printed in 1516. Though in the end he remained loyal to the Roman Church, Erasmus's influence on all the reformers was so great that it has been said that "Erasmus laid the egg that Luther hatched." All sought to improve the accuracy of the biblical translations by getting behind the Latin Vulgate version of the Bible dating from the time of Jerome in the early fifth century. Such activity broke the clergy's monopoly on reading Holy Writ and interpreting it to the ignorant masses. It was a major step towards putting the Bible in the hands of the people, for Martin Luther soon translated it into German, Jacques Lefèvre into French, Olavus Petri into Swedish, William Tyndale, Miles Coverdale, Richard Taverner, and a host of others into English.

For the sake of convenience, the movements collectively known as the Reformation are usually divided into four major strands: the Lutheran reform in Germany and Scandinavia; the Calvinist reform in Switzerland, Germany, France, and the Low Countries; the Anabaptist reform in Germany, Switzerland, Eastern Europe, and the Low Countries; and the Anglican reform of Henry VIII in England. A closer look at the life and work of Martin Luther will shed much light on the nature of Protestant reform. Luther is in relation to the Reformation like the opening notes of a great piano concerto—first the theme is stated, then in turn it is taken up by other instruments, and finally it is lost in the developing pattern of music. Surely the Reformation would have occurred without Martin Luther, but what happened in this man's private soul affected the direction of a great religious movement involving millions of people.

Luther was a monk and tried his best to be a good one. In the beginning he did not set out to reform the Church, but simply tried to make sure that God looked on him with favor. He was terrified by the righteousness of God, which meant to him the judgment of Christ and the wrath of God if his law was not kept. To meet these demands, Luther fasted until his cheeks caved in, punished himself mentally and physically for his gnawing sense of unworthiness, and confessed every sin he could think of—to the point that his spiritual father in the monastery, Johann Staupitz, finally told him, "God is not angry with you; you are angry with him. Why don't you commit a terrible sin like murder or fornication so that he will have something to forgive?" Through Staupitz, Luther was appointed the professor of Bible in the new University of Wittenberg, and it was in preparing his lectures on Psalms, Romans, Galatians, and Hebrews that he realized that no one can stand before God unless first one be called by God, forgiven and healed through the suffering, love, and power of Christ. What a person must do, Luther discovered, is simply believe and trust in what God has already done in Christ. This is the meaning of what Paul said—that we are saved by grace through the gift of faith and not by works. The New Testament teaching of "justification by grace through faith" (Romans 1:17) became a keynote of the Reformation.

We have already mentioned (in connection with the Crusades) the matter of indulgences, granted by the Church in return for payment or services. Indulgences released one (or one's relatives and friends who had died) from so many years in purgatory by transferring to them the extra goodness of the saints. This "extra goodness" was known as the "treasury of merit," an accumulation of the overabundant merit or credit of Christ, the Virgin Mary, and the saints of the Church. This practice troubled an increasing number of people because of its potential for corruption, and soon Luther was horrified that indulgences were being used to raise money for the new St. Peter's Cathedral in Rome in exchange for a blanket forgiveness of sins. It perverted the very essence of Luther's recent discovery: only God can forgive sin; forgiveness cannot be bought, sold, or dispensed by the Church. The Reformation was launched in earnest when Luther protested by posting his Niney-five Theses for debate on the door of the Wittenberg church on October 31, 1517. The printing presses soon spread them all over Germany, and in time Pope Leo X had to acknowledge that there was "a wild boar in the vineyard."

By the end of 1520, Luther had fully developed his Reformation principles in debates and treatises, and was excommunicated by Rome. He reduced the seven sacraments of the Roman Church to two—baptism and the Lord's Supper. He not only translated all of Scripture into German, but wrote hymns and new liturgies so that people could understand and participate in worship. He wrote catechisms and simple songs to help children learn the basics of the faith. He denied the division of status between pastors and people, asserting the priesthood of all believers and developing a theology of vocation, which stressed God's call to ministry regardless of one's task in life. He elevated Scripture to the highest authority over any church, pope, council, or tradition. He called for the closing of monasteries and said that monks, nuns, and priests should be free to marry. Baptism done in faith, for Luther, was the only vow of the Christian, not those added by monastics—poverty, chastity, and obedience. Luther himself married a remarkable former nun, Katherine von Bora, and the example of their lively and happy home set a model for young pastors. It was the attempt to follow the teachings of the Bible that led Luther to give up many practices of the Roman Catholic Church, and it is with his reform that we can speak most accurately and historically of the evangelical principles of Protestantism.

Luther's Reformation was only one of many. The blast from his trumpet aroused many throughout Europe to the cause of reforming their own churches. The work of Swiss reformers especially had far-reaching effects. Begun in Zürich during the 1520s by Huldrich Zwingli, the most complete program of reform came from the genius of John Calvin, a second generation reformer who was the leader in Geneva between 1541 and his death in 1564. The adherents of Calvin's "Reformed" theology (the name applied to that tradition) stressed the greatness and majesty of God, placed more of a direct emphasis on the activity of the Holy Spirit (especially among Puritans), promoted the idea of a pure visible church of professing believers with detailed structures of authority and discipline, urged a godly preaching and teaching ministry in all churches, and reminded the civil leaders of their ordained responsibility to keep order according to God's moral law.

'One Body . . . Many Members'

Protestant refugees from all over Europe congregated in the Swiss city-states and later took the "Reformed" tenets back to their own countries—the most notable being the English Puritans, who, in time, temporarily abolished the episcopal Church of England (because of its "popish" practices), executed a king, and left an indelible imprint on America through their New England settlements. The Presbyterian and Congregational churches trace their origins to Calvin and English Puritanism. Baptists find their earliest kin in the "Anabaptists" (meaning to rebaptize) who first went beyond Zwingli's more cautious reform in Zürich and then spread quickly throughout Europe, being persecuted wherever they went. This radical wing of the Reformation rejected infant baptism, separated their churches totally from the state, forsook oaths and military service, and generally were disconcerting to moderate Protestants and Catholics alike (Luther accused the radicals of having swallowed the Holy Spirit, feathers and all). Countless men, women, and children gave their lives for these dissenting beliefs. Today the Anabaptist tradition is seen in the historic "peace churches" such as the Mennonites. More accurately, those whom we now identify as Baptists trace their historical roots directly to the more radical wing of English Separatist Puritanism during the first half of the seventeenth century.

The Evangelical Covenant Church is rooted both in the work of the magisterial reformers, especially Luther, and the principles of the free church tradition of believers' churches, articulated first by the left-wing reformers and then by English Puritans. The Swedish Reformation was totally Lutheran in character, its leader, Olavus Petri, having been a student at Wittenberg during the eventful months prior to the Ninety-five Theses. So we see that the Covenant is a child of the Reformation, and that we need to study with care and appreciation the riches of that tradition.

THE EVANGELICAL AWAKENINGS

The Evangelical Covenant Church traces its origins more directly to the period during the eighteenth and nineteenth centuries when spiritual renewal swept through most Protestant groups in Europe and America, leading in many cases to the formation of new churches and denominations. Many believed that Protestant churches were now in need of their own reformation as cold formalism and heavy emphasis on right doctrine seemed to drain all life and spirit. It was during this time that such leading movements as Pietism and Methodism emerged, stressing personal conversion and holy living, and shaping structures that would encourage those in the faith to grow and serve and be sensitive to fresh winds of the Spirit.

The period known as the modern Church, from the close of the Reformation to the present, is a complex time of the further fragmentation of Protestantism in a series of social, political, intellectual, and industrial revolutions as Western nations have struggled to assert their power and independence. Scientific discoveries and new intellectual currents have swept across the civilized world, challenging the Church in unprecedented ways. Since this relatively long period of time has so many facets, we will confine ourselves to those movements which have most profoundly affected the Evangelical Covenant Church.

Following the brilliant and dynamic thought of the first generation reformers, the Reformation churches sought to preserve the teaching of their respective founders by rigidly defining orthodoxy in confessional statements. The toleration of other churches was a burning issue. In Germany, for example, the Peace of Augsburg (1555) officially recognized only Lutheranism and Roman Catholicism. The fact that other major churches were excluded, Calvin's "Reformed" churches among them, resulted in continued strife that contributed in large part to the Thirty Years' War (1618-1648) which devastated much of Europe. By 1580, Lutherans had defined their doctrine in the *Book of Concord*—which comprised the Augsburg Confession (1530), the small and large catechisms of Luther, the Formula of Concord (1577), and other creedal statements. While it brought some peace to Lutheran in-fighting, it also elevated other documents besides the Bible to standards of orthodoxy. Likewise, the Reformed theology of Calvin was variously consolidated in the Scottish Confession (1560), the Belgic Confession (1561), the Heidelberg Catechism (1562), the Second Helvetic (Swiss) Confession (1566), and eventually the famous Westminster Confession (1648). This movement has been labeled Protestant Scholasticism, a name that signifies a heavy emphasis on right belief and intellectual assent. Ironically, the Protestant Church largely succumbed to the very spirit of rigidity and lifelessness which it had resisted a century earlier, but such cycles are not uncommon in the ongoing life of the Church.

As in earlier times, fresh movements of renewal arose to challenge prevailing beliefs and practices. The evangelical awakenings of the eighteenth century are seen in the Pietists of Germany, the Methodists—followers of John Wesley—in England, and the Great Awakenings in the American colonies. In the judgment of many, these saved the Christian Church from both stultification and secularization during a time when Protestant Scholasticism was still entrenched in the major church traditions, and when the Enlightenment spirit was giving birth to religious skepticism and to philosophies such as Deism, which emphasized independent human reason and branded the virgin birth, miracles, and the resurrection as fantastic myths, necessary only to support the faith of the weak. But the Enlightenment also bequeathed positive gains in culture and religion. Its campaign against superstition largely put an end to magic and witchcraft trials which were so widespread in seventeenth-century Protestant lands. The ideal of natural law as a basis for a universal ethic and the ideal of free humanity continue to this day to distinguish Western democracies from the oppressive totalitarianism of the twentieth century in many countries.

The Evangelical Covenant Church has grown out of the movement known as Pietism. Its chief characteristics (and those of other groups of the Awakening, for that matter) are that it is experiential, emotional, individual, Bible centered, and ethically minded. It gives primacy to feeling in religious experience, to a personal, living relationship with Christ through conversion. The head, the Pietist demands, must descend into the heart. Whereas the Orthodox would ask, "Are you sound?" the Pietist would ask, "Are you saved?" For this reason historic Pietism has been one of the least understood movements, with critics leveling charges of legalism and subjectivism. This has been the case particularly in America, where the term *pietism* is often construed to mean a kind of Victorian prudishness or false piety. This, fortunately, is changing as a growing understanding and appreciation of the movement is breaking down inaccurate stereotypes.

Historically, Pietism is usually associated with the movement in Germany led by Philip Jacob Spener and August Hermann Francke. Conventicles (groups meeting informally for worship and fellowship outside the church—usually in the home) began gathering in 1670 under Spener's leadership in Frankfurt-am-Main, where he was pastor of the state Lutheran church from 1666 to 1686. Besides having read widely in Puritan literature and devotional treatises, early Pietists were influenced further by the mysticism of writers like Johann Arndt and his pupil Paul Gerhardt, the great Lutheran hymnwriter. In 1675, Spener challenged the Lutheran territorial church system by writing a lengthy introduction to a new edition of Arndt's *True Christianity* (1605-09), which was soon published separately as *Pia Desideria,* a Latin phrase meaning pious desires or wishes. In an attempt to recover the pristine teachings of Luther, Spener offered six proposals which describe the essence of Pietism: 1) intensified study of the Bible; 2) the spiritual priesthood of the laity; 3) the spirit of love—the practical side of the Christian faith (as Francke said, "I would rather have a drop of true love than an ocean of knowledge"); 4) charity in controversy; 5) reorganization of theological studies in the universities with higher standards of religious life (to this end the University of Halle was organized in 1694); and 6) the reform of preaching and the encouragement of an awakened ministry.

'One Body . . . Many Members'

Spener formed his *collegia pietatis* (small conventicles) to realize this program; the groups were not intended to separate from the state church, but to work quietly within it to breathe new life into established structures. Soon, with the help of Francke, other institutions were created: a pauper school, a boys' boarding school, an orphanage, a Latin school, a printing press, a pharmacy, and a Bible institute which trained 6,000 ministers and missionaries. An important wing of the Pietist movement was the Moravians, led by Count Nicholas von Zinzendorf and influenced by the Bohemian Brethren, who had an even more heightened spirituality and communal spirit. The Moravians energetically sent missionaries throughout the world and influenced in a profound way John Wesley and the Methodist revivals in England during the 1740s, and, in conjunction with the Methodists, were instrumental in bringing the evangelical awakening to Sweden in the nineteenth century. As a result, those who became known as "Mission Friends" during the Swedish revivals in those years were especially characterized by the "heart religion" of the Moravians. This stressed a personal relationship to the crucified and risen Christ, whose completed work on the cross was the basis not for gloom and pious introspection but for joy and celebration.

Swede Bend, Iowa

THE COVENANT CHURCH IN NORTH AMERICA

When the Swedish Mission Friends came to America in the late nineteenth century, they left a homogeneous religious and cultural envelope only to encounter the most diverse country and people in the world. As they created new lives for themselves, the faith of these Swedes was strengthened and their Christian outreach found new expressions. But as this fledgling church grew, it also was shaped by its interaction with American culture and its plethora of religious traditions. This experience contains today as well, as third and fourth generation Covenanters endeavor to maintain a vital witness that is true to the heritage handed down by their ancestors, whether that lineage be in the faith or in the flesh.

This is not the place to tell the full story of the birth and adolescence of the Covenant Church in Sweden and North America, for that has been clearly detailed in the church's denominational histories (see "Suggestions for Further Reading" below). But the Mission Friends who came to the United States and Canada to forge new lives for themselves and their families encountered a challenging religious and social milieu unlike anything they had known in Sweden. While they had been accustomed to a homogeneous ecclesiastical environment in the homeland—the State Lutheran Church—Swedish Pietism in the new country became just another ingredient in the ethnic and denominational salad bowl of American religion. This movement in Sweden of the Spirit of God, which was more along the lines of a happening than an institutional church, confronted many forces as an immigrant body in North America. These have left their marks on an identity which is even yet in the process of emerging.

We have seen that the Swedish Mission friends were nurtured in a Lutheran environment which was rooted in the sole authority of Scripture, valued the historic creeds of the early Church and the teachings of the Fathers, and looked to the substance and vitality of Luther's understanding of faith, worship, and the Christian life; all provided focus for their theological and liturgical expression. But these Swedes were also Pietists who traced their pedigree to the dissenting movements of all ages: the introspection and ecstacy of the mystics; the courage of the left-wing reformers who fought for their believers' churches and the rights of individual Christian conscience and freedom; the spirituality of the great Puritan divines; the "heart religion" of the Moravians and the Methodists—all trying to resuscitate with the new life of the Spirit churches which they believed were increasingly comatose. In a way rather difficult to describe, these early Mission Friends stood in both a "catholic" and a "free church" tradition as seen through the eyes of the Reformation.

In brief, this is the spiritual home the first Covenanters brought with them to North America. When the Evangelical Covenant Church was organized in Chicago in 1885, it became one of many denominations in the United States—a phenomenon especially peculiar to this country, though increasingly a pattern throughout the Western Church since the seventeenth century. Today there are about 240 denominations and, some estimate, upwards of 900 separate religious groups in the United States. Inevitably, the Covenant has had to stretch as it has grown from infancy to maturity in such a setting. The early Covenanters discovered a natural affinity to the revival movements in America, which had a deep and diverse tradition all their own. It was only natural that much of the substance and many of the techniques would find their way into segments of the Covenant. Some became intrigued with the age-old millenarian speculation of how the world would end and when Christ would return. Others argued about the extent to which the Mission Friends movement should be organized into a denomination with central leadership. When the scientific theories of the past century and the rise of higher biblical criticism posed threats to certain views of faith and the Bible, some Covenanters took sides in the debates between "modernists" and "fundamentalists" on such issues as evolution, biblical inerrancy, the atonement, and eschatology. Others became involved in ecumenical discussions and movements for peace and social justice.

Despite such growing diversity within the ranks, however, the Covenant has remained firmly bound to its fundamental principle of theological freedom, testing all things by the written Word of God, giving intellectual and spiritual liberty to the consciences of all who are united together by a vital personal relationship with Jesus Christ, yet subject to the common wisdom of the church. Like all immigrant churches, the Covenant's original ethnicity— its "Swedishness"—is passing with each generation. It is a growing church, eager to extend the right hand of fellowship to all who come to its doors confessing Christ and seeking the warmth of a church home. The backgrounds and religious orientation of its new members are many, and the challenge is great to grow and change while still maintaining the biblical and historic essentials which form the basis of its identity. The Covenant Church is more diverse today than it ever has been, and with that comes crucial and unforseen responsibilities in its life together.

Our name says much about the nature of the Evangelical Covenant Church. The word "evangelical" indicates its spirit of commitment to the good news of God's forgiveness offered to all persons in Jesus Christ, not a fixed list of doctrines. The word "covenant" indicates its principle of voluntary association for the purpose of engaging in the work of the Kingdom of God. The Covenant has no formulated creed but holds to the Protestant principle of the authority of the Scriptures, and to the primacy of the fellowship of believers rooted in the living voice of the Spirit in the Church through the ages—a voice which it must continue to hear and allow to speak through it to future generations. We need to know not only our place in the long history of the Christian Church, but also that we are part of its ongoing history. What started with the apostles does not conclude with us. The Covenant is not the end result of what began with the primitive fellowship in Jerusalem. Rather, the Church—and our Covenant— is a place where we all begin.

SUGGESTIONS FOR FURTHER READING

For those who wish to investigate more fully the general history of the Church or particular aspects of it, the following list of books would be a good place to begin. All are still in print.

General Church History

Williston Walker, *A History of the Christian Church*, Scribners, 3rd edition, 1970. Edited by Cyril C. Richardson, Wilhelm Pauck, and Robert T. Handy.

First published in 1918, this book has long been the standard work on the subject and is still used in most seminary church history surveys. It is especially useful for its detailed comprehensiveness. It is available only in hard cover.

Roland Bainton, *Christendom: A Short History of Christianity and Its Impact on Western Civilization*, 2 volumes, Harper and Row, 1964, 1966.

This two volume paperback is perhaps the best introduction for the person who knows little of the Church's history. It is written in a lively style and is generously illustrated with examples of Christian art from each period. It is a pleasure for anyone to read.

Bruce L. Shelley, *Church History in Plain Language*, Word Books, 1982.

This paperback is more substantial than its title suggests. It is a detailed history of the Church, yet written in a style well-suited to the person with little background. The book contains several useful maps, charts, and diagrams to illustrate the text.

The Pelican History of the Church, a collection of inexpensive paperbacks, is the best series, written by outstanding scholars in their fields. Each is available separately.

1) Henry Chadwick, *The Early Church*, Penguin Books, 1967.

2) R.W. Southern, *Western Society and the Church in the Middle Ages*, Penguin Books, 1970.

3) Owen Chadwick, *The Reformation*, Penguin Books, 1964.

4) G.R. Cragg, *The Church and the Age of Reason, 1648-1789*, Penguin Books, 1960.

5) Alec R. Vidler, *The Church in an Age of Revolution*, Penguin Books, 1961.

6) Stephen Neill, *A History of Christian Missions*, Penguin Books, 1964.

American Church History

Winthrop S. Hudson, *Religion in America*, Scribners, 3rd edition, 1981.
First published in 1965, this has become the most widely used text on American church history. Those who wish to learn more about the complex and fascinating story of American religion will find this a helpful book. It is available in paperback.

Sydney E. Ahlstrom, *A Religious History of the American People*, Yale University Press, 1972.
This massive yet extremely readable survey of American religion is more broad in its scope than Hudson's work. Ahlstrom goes beyond the major denominations to describe America's fascinating mosaic of sects and popular religion. It is available in paperback.

Covenant History

Karl A. Olsson, *By One Spirit*, Covenant Press, 1962.
This is the definitive and detailed history of the Evangelical Covenant Church. It is essential reading for anyone who wishes to study in-depth the story of the church. It is available in paperback.

Karl A. Olsson, *A Family of Faith: Ninety Years of Covenant History*, Covenant Press, 1975.
An anniversary volume, this is a shorter popular history of the Covenant which, in part, brings up-to-date Dr. Olsson's earlier history of the church. This is in paperback.

Glenn P. Anderson, ed., *Covenant Roots: Sources and Affirmations*, Covenant Press, 1980.

This is an interesting and instructive collection of some of the important sermons, essays, and organizational records of the early Covenant. It is available in paperback.

Donald C. Frisk, *Covenant Affirmations: This We Believe*, Covenant Press, 1981.

This paperback volume, written by the emeritus professor of theology at North Park Theological Seminary, is an excellent introduction to the faith and practice of the Evangelical Covenant Church. A brief booklet, also entitled "Covenant Affirmations" and available from Covenant Press, summarizes what the Covenant believes and what is developed more fully by Professor Frisk in this major study.

David Nyvall, *My Father's Testament*, Covenant Press, 1974.

This translation by Eric G. Hawkinson of a book originally published in Swedish in 1924, has been hailed as the "most important source book for our early history." It is David Nyvall's (the first president of North Park College and Seminary) interpretation of his father's diary. C.J. Nyvall was one of the leading lay leaders of the revival in Sweden and instrumental in the formation of the Covenant in both Sweden and America. It captures the mood and experience of the early Covenant in a unique way. It is available in paperback.